Original title:
Tales from the Ocean's Edge

Copyright © 2025 Creative Arts Management OÜ
All rights reserved.

Author: Benjamin Caldwell
ISBN HARDBACK: 978-1-80587-000-6
ISBN PAPERBACK: 978-1-80587-939-8

Heartstrings of the Ocean

A crab in a tux, looking quite grand,
With a bow tie so neat, he's the talk of the sand.
He dances on rocks, with his pincers held high,
While seagulls all squawk, watching him fly.

A starfish named Larry, quite lazy and bright,
Dreams of being a diver, oh what a sight!
He flips through the waves, with a bubble or two,
While fish laugh and giggle, 'What's wrong with you?'

A clam at the party, so shy and so sweet,
Got sand in his shell, and it's hard to compete.
He jokes with a seaweed, both green and quite brash,
"Let's open a restaurant, we'll serve up a splash!"

The dolphins are leaping, with laughter and grace,
But one snags a buoy, now stuck in a race!
With flips and with flops, they all start to cheer,
"Just hope he won't splash—oh no, he's right here!"

So under the sun, with all of their cheer,
The critters of the coast bring us joy every year.
With laughter and fun, from the water to shore,
Life near the waves is never a bore!

Chronicles of the Lost Harbor

Oh, I once met a crab named Lou,
He danced like a drunk on the sand, it's true.
He lost his left claw in a quarrel with fate,
Now he claps to the beat, it's a real funny gait.

The seagulls all laughed, they couldn't get enough,
As Lou showed off moves that were quite, quite tough.
He stumbled and tumbled and fell on his face,
The tide rolled in giggling, it joined the race.

Where Sea Meets Sky

The fish above thought they could fly,
While dolphins below were ready to try.
A whale made a splash and called out, "Dive in!"
The gulls, quite disgruntled, shouted, "Let's spin!"

Crabs threw a party, it was quite a sight,
With shrimp serving tea, oh what a delight!
They danced on the waves with a splash and a cheer,
"Who needs a boat when we've got this here?"

The Nautical Muse

A wise old octopus scribbled in ink,
On seaweed scrolls he would put down his think.
He penned tales of ships that were lost in the mist,
But most of his verses just ended up missed.

The mermaids would giggle, they read what he wrote,
About a fish dressed as a pirate afloat.
His humor was salty, his rhymes were quite wide,
With sea-life adventures, he took them for a ride.

Memories within the Mariner's Compass

In a bottle sat Bob, the forgetful old squid,
He'd point left for fish, but right as he slid.
The compass would spin, and the fish gave a wink,
As Bob lost his way to the jellyfish drink.

He visited corals that flipped into glee,
Called out to the crabs, "Come sing along, three!"
With a tap dance of bubbles, they twirled all around,
Creating such chaos, that laughter just drowned.

Heartbeats in the Sand

Footprints chased by waves so spry,
A crab in a tux, oh my oh my!
Seagulls squawk with jokes to spread,
As beach balls bounce above our head.

A sandy dog with a stick so grand,
Digging deep like he's got a plan.
Laughter spills like ocean's foam,
In this silly, sun-kissed home.

The Echoing Shell

I found a shell, so shiny and bright,
Listening close, it gave me a fright.
A voice inside said, "It's snack time!"
But turned out it just liked to rhyme.

I asked the shell for life advice,
It talked about fish and being nice.
But when I asked for a joke or two,
It clammed right up, and I said, "Boo!"

Shadows of the Incoming Tide

The shadows stretch in playful dance,
A jellyfish invites us for a prance.
But he's a bit clumsy, stings us with glee,
"Try not to trip over me!" says he.

A starfish laughs, stuck on a rock,
He tells a joke that makes the waves mock.
We tumble and giggle in the soft sea glow,
With shadows of laughter, to and fro.

The Solitary Lighthouse

A lighthouse stands, all alone on the coast,
He winks at sailors like a playful ghost.
At night he blinks in a rhythm most strange,
"Just checking the light, I'm a bit deranged!"

With a grin, he spins, then forgets his place,
Lighting up the waves in a game of chase.
He beams so bright when the fog rolls in,
"Hurry up, boats! Let the fun begin!"

Lighthouses in the Gloaming

A lighthouse stood all proud and tall,
Guiding lost ships with a wobbly call.
But in the haze of the gloaming light,
It learned to dance in the wind's delight.

With a beam that winked like a cheeky grin,
It played hide and seek with a seagull's kin.
The barnacles laughed, and the waves did sway,
As the lighthouse jiggled in its own merry play.

Seaglass Memories

On a beach where the sand meets the cheer,
Seaglass whispers secrets loud and clear.
Every shard a story, some funny, some bold,
Of washed-up pirates and treasures untold.

A round piece chuckled of a fishy guy,
Who wore a shell hat and could fly (oh my!).
While a jagged green shard had tales of a shoe,
That danced with a crab in the sun's golden hue.

The Daughter of the Turquoise Depths

She swam in hues of blues and greens,
With bubbles of laughter and jellybean dreams.
The fish would giggle as she twirled round,
A graceful splash, then a plop on the ground.

She'd pull on a seaweed and make it her crown,
While crabs did the cha-cha, up and down.
With a flip of her fin, she could make quite a scene,
To the tune of a clam, she would burst out in sheen.

The Quietude Before the Storm

In the hush of the sea, as the sky turned gray,
A clam sat tight, at what fate would play.
The gulls were plotting some mischief afloat,
While a storm whistled soft like a cat on a coat.

The turtles held meetings with plans quite absurd,
To tickle the thunder or give the wind a word.
With a wink from the wave, and a giggle so grand,
They braced for the splash, oh, do you understand?

Colors of the Ocean's Heart

Blue like a fish with a big froggy grin,
Red like the crab who's an expert in sin.
Green seaweed sways with a silly little dance,
While purple fish giggle, they can't miss a chance.

Yellow sunbeams tickle the ocean's fine face,
Orange seashells hide in a whimsical place.
The coral laughs loudly, a vibrant parade,
As colors collide in this watery charade.

The Wind's Embrace

The wind whispers softly, a tickle in flight,
Sailing dreams through the day and into the night.
It plays with the waves, a game of charades,
As seagulls make faces in wind-blown cascades.

Fishermen chuckle, their nets full of air,
While the breeze ties a knot in the captain's wild hair.
The ocean giggles as boats start to swing,
Caught in a waltz by the wind's silly fling.

Stories Carried by the Driftwood

Driftwood tells secrets, with grins carved in bark,
Of crabs that throw parties, oh what a lark!
Barnacles gossip, their shells all aglow,
While starfish throw stars in the shoreline show.

Once a plank was a pirate, or maybe a bench,
Now it dreams of the waves with a salty old wrench.
Wooden tales tumble, rolling along sand,
Each with a punchline that's perfectly planned.

The Anemone's Tale

An anemone winks with a fluttering grace,
Tickling the clownfish who joins in the race.
With tentacles waving, a comical sight,
As fish giggle madly, what a silly night!

"Come dance with me, shrimp!" the anemone calls,
"Let's swirl in the bubbles and dodge the big squalls."
While sea urchins chuckle from their prickly nests,
Swapping funny tales that make their friends jest.

Legends of the Saltwater Realm

A crab named Clyde wore a crown,
He marched through sand, his royal gown.
The fish all laughed, the dolphins played,
While Clyde just strutted, unafraid.

A clam that dreamed of being bold,
Swapped shells with a clam that was old.
But stories told of crabs so grand,
Left clams debating on the sand.

A turtle slow, with style and flair,
Wore shades and claimed to have no care.
He flipped and flopped, and turned around,
While fish just giggled, splashing ground.

In every wave, a giggle floats,
A sea of chuckles, lively notes.
With every splash and every tide,
The salty realm does laugh and glide.

The Unseen Dancer of the Deep

A shadow swayed beneath the sea,
With tentacles long, it danced for free.
The fish all watched with jaws agape,
While bubbles popped in silly shape.

An octopus with eight left feet,
Tried tangoing with crabs to greet.
They laughed so hard, they lost the beat,
And wiggled on, a twisted feat.

A starfish raved on stony floor,
With arms stretched wide, it craved for more.
But every twist, a clumsy turn,
Had all the fish begin to yearn.

Beneath the waves, where laughter spins,
The unseen dancer surely wins.
For life beneath, though dark it seems,
Is filled with joy and funny dreams.

Whispers in the Mist

A seagull perched upon a beam,
Spoke tales of waves as if a dream.
"Did you hear," it said with glee,
"The fish can talk, just like you and me?"

The oysters chomped and heard the word,
And laughed so hard, they barely stirred.
"The fish?" they said, "Oh, what a treat,
They swim in circles, ain't that sweet?"

A blowfish puffed with pride so great,
Claimed to know all, had much to state.
But when he boasted, puffed too wide,
And all the crabs began to slide.

In misty air, the stories flow,
With whispers soft, and giggles low.
For all that dwells where waters kiss,
Enjoys a laugh, a salty bliss.

A Journey Through Coral Shadows

In coral caves, a fish set out,
To find new worlds, to swim about.
With goggles on, a pearl so bright,
He dove through shadows, full of light.

A hermit crab gave quite a chase,
He scolded fish with grumpy grace.
"Get off my lawn!" he wiggled fine,
While fish just giggled, "You're so divine!"

A snail on shells moved ever slow,
Declared, "With speed, I'm quite the show!"
The fish zoomed past with tails unfurled,
While snails just sighed, "This is my world."

Through coral paths, where laughter rings,
The sea's alive with happy flings.
For every shadow, light breaks through,
In journeys full of laughs anew.

The Tide's Gentle Spell

The tide pulls back, a funny sight,
With starfish dancing in the light.
A crab just laughs, then scuttles fast,
Saying, "I'm late, I'll be a blast!"

Seagulls squawk with comic flair,
Stealing chips from folks who stare.
A beach ball rolls on sandy shores,
And bounces back for encore roars!

Wet feet chase a giggling breeze,
Waves break with laughter, oh what tease!
Sandcastles tumble, so it seems,
But kings of sand have silly dreams!

As sunset paints the sky with glee,
Dancing shadows come to see.
The ocean smiles, a gentle jest,
Inviting all to join the fest!

The Fisherman's Promise

A fisherman with luck so grand,
Swears fish will jump right in his hand.
His friends just snicker, roll their eyes,
"Last week you caught just seashell sighs!"

He casts his line, the bait looks fine,
But all he catches are chats with brine.
"Just wait!" he shouts, "The big one's near!"
A fish jumps high—it's just a sphere!

His net is full, or so he claims,
Yet all he's got are fishy games.
He spins a yarn, his tales so tall,
But all his fish are not that small!

At last he catches a flat old shoe,
Laced with stories, one or two.
Winking at sharks that swim beneath,
He laughs and promises more of this!

Skimming Stones and Whispered Wishes

We gathered stones, smooth and round,
To skim across the water's sound.
With every toss, a wish we'd make,
"Please let my life be one big cake!"

But every stone would flip and flop,
And make a splash with every drop.
"Hey, stop that, you pesky stone!"
Said one who wanted wishes grown!

The tide just giggled, gave a grin,
As waves kept whispering thick and thin.
A stone collected dreams of sand,
While one just wet a very hand!

At sunset's call, our wishes flew,
The sea embraced the laughter too.
With every ripple, we all smiled—
Our hearts as light as dreams reviled!

Shores of Forgotten Echoes

On shores where echoes hide and peek,
We heard the jokes that waves did speak.
A dolphin popped and waved with glee,
"Why so serious? Come play with me!"

Old shells would chime with stories told,
Of mermaids dance and pirates bold.
But truth be told, they looked so daft,
We couldn't help but break with laughter's craft!

Crashing waves would mimic sighs,
As seagulls plotted goofy skies.
Each flap a dance, each dive a trick,
Making us laugh till time was slick.

So here we stand, 'mid echoes bright,
With salty air and hearts so light.
In every laugh the ocean shares,
We find our joy, free of cares!

Journey to the Blackened Rock

On a quest to find that famed black stone,
Captain Chuck slipped and cried, "Oh no!"
His shipmates laughed, they knew the score,
"You'll find it lost among the floor!"

With nets and snacks, they set their sail,
The wind was great, but oh, the gale!
"I'm not afraid!" said Sally with cheer,
"Unless we meet a kraken near!"

Past fish that giggle, and crabs that dance,
They threw a party, gave joy a chance.
A mermaid popped up with fries and shakes,
"Join us, dear sailors, for life's no mistake!"

They weaved through storms, over waves so bright,
With slapstick antics that brought pure delight.
Though the blackened rock still remained a myth,
They'd found enough laughter, no need for a fifth!

Ebb and Flow: A Maritime Diary

In the morning mist where the seagulls squawk,
A sailor wrote on a wobbling dock.
He penned of tides that seemed to play,
"Why did the fish leave? I'm lost today!"

With a rhyming pen and an off-key tune,
The ocean danced under a silly moon.
"Dear diary," he scribbled with flair,
"My compass points north, but I'm going somewhere!"

The crabs held meetings with a mighty plan,
To take over the beach, oh, what a clan!
But instead, they danced and marched so wrong,
While the sailor chuckled, "Now that's my song!"

When the tide rolled in with a crash and a splash,
He laughed as his papers went off in a flash.
Yet every wave whispered secrets so deep,
In the ebb and flow, bright memories sleep!

Lost Ships and Oceanic Whispers

A ship once sailed with a crew full of dreams,
But all they found were far-off screams.
"Is that a ghost?" asked the cook with dread,
"Or just the dinner we forgot to be fed?"

With every whisper from the deep blue sea,
The sailor scratched his head and said, "Is it me?"
He listened closely, heard secrets unfold,
"Stay away from the anchors—a tale retold!"

Ghost ships sailed by with their sails all askew,
And the captain snickered, "What else is new?"
They waved at phantoms, shared fishy jokes,
As lost ships giggled with ancient folks.

Ultimately, they docked on a sandy shore,
With stories so silly, who could ask for more?
By moonlight's glow, they shared their delight,
As laughter echoed through the starry night!

The Dance of the Jellyfish

Under water where the jellyfish sway,
A party's brewing, come join the ballet!
With wobbly moves, oh, how they twirl,
Inviting the fish for a glimmering whirl.

The octopus played on a makeshift drum,
While a clam squeaked out a jazzy hum.
"Let's groove!" cried a crab, "I'll lead the way,
To the rhythm of waves, let's all play!"

A starfish spun with glittering grace,
While all around joined the underwater race.
"Who knew," said a shrimp, "such fun could be found,
In the dance of the sea, where joy knows no bound?"

As bubbles rose high, the moonlight shone,
The creatures of night, they danced alone.
In the ocean so vast, with laughter abloom,
The jellyfish twirled to their watery tune!

Constellations of the Sea

Starfish gather for a show,
Their wobbly dance steals the glow.
A crab recites a funny rhyme,
Underwater jokes, oh so fine!

The jellyfish wear their best hats,
Floating by in silly spats.
Octopus plays the ukulele,
Bubbles burst—oh what a ballet!

Seahorses trot in parade line,
Whispering secrets, quite divine.
They giggle and toss about,
In this sea of fun, we shout!

The fish dive deep to steal the show,
With pirouettes in a funny flow.
As waves applaud this ocean spree,
We laugh—'What a sight to see!'

The Ethereal Dance of the Kelp

Kelp sways gently, quite the tease,
With tangled limbs that wiggle with ease.
A fish tries to tango, lost its way,
Each twirl a comedy, hip-hip-hooray!

Barnacles gossip on a stone,
Chiming in like they're on loan.
They burst into laughter, giving glee,
To the rhythm of waves and dappled sea.

A sea lion joins in the dance,
Jumps and rolls, oh what a prance!
With laughter echoing throughout the tide,
The ocean's heart, full of pride.

And as the moon smiles from up high,
The creatures wink in the night sky.
Each sway a sign, let's spin and play,
In this underwater cabaret!

A Clockwork of Shells

Shells align, their colors bright,
Each one clicks, a musical sight.
The starfish plays the triangle loud,
While snails form up a quirky crowd!

Turtles tumble with a spin,
Their laughter bubbles from within.
Clams chime in with a rhythmic clap,
Together creating a seaside map.

The conch shell sings an opera tune,
While crabs dance like it's a boon.
All working in this underwater crew,
Though some get stuck like they always do!

As the tide rolls in, the laughter flows,
In this shell clock, where time just glows.
Each tick and tock brings joy and cheer,
In the comedic world of water near!

Stories in the Wake

Ripples tell tales, waves laugh and play,
Fish whisper secrets in a bubbly relay.
A dolphin giggles, leaps in the spray,
Making the ocean better each day!

Seagulls squawk with comic flair,
Diving for tidbits without a care.
Their antics bring giggles and sighs,
As they swoop and play in the skies.

A turtle slowly joins the fun,
Wobbling along, it's never done.
Judging each splash with a side-eye glance,
In this watery world, all take a chance!

With every wave, the humor's alive,
In the ocean's wake, all creatures thrive.
In this funny dance beneath the sun,
Where laughter and joy forever run!

Fishermen's Soliloquy

The fish they dance, the bait's a trap,
But Timmy swears he's found a map.
With every cast, a tale unfolds,
Of seaweed monsters, treasures gold.

A crab stole lunch, oh what a heist,
He'll miss his sandwich day or night.
With every wave a laugh erupts,
While gulls plot ways to steal our cups.

The sun sets low, but spirits rise,
As fish tell stories of their lies.
A tarpon jumps, he bids adieu,
With every splash, we laugh anew.

In this odd world, where fish swim free,
We find our truths, as we agree.
With nets and jokes, our hearts beyond,
We sail away, our laughter's bond.

Under the Coral Canopy

A clownfish grins with paint so bright,
He cracks a joke, it's quite a sight.
"Why did the coral blush?" he said,
"Because it saw the ocean bed!"

With turtles slow, and dolphins spry,
They giggle as they swim on by.
A seaweed dance, oh what a scene,
This underwater world's too keen.

The octopus dons a funny hat,
He waves his arms, "Come sit and chat!"
"Did you hear about the shrimp so bold?
He stole a wave, but left the gold!"

Beneath the waves, where laughter flows,
Anemones sway, play hide and show.
In this bright world, we share our glee,
With every bubble, pure ecstasy.

Riddles of the Rolling Surf

The waves roll in with the tide's quick breath,
Whispers of laughter, tales of jest.
"What did the ocean say to the shore?"
"Stop waving at me, I'm quite in score!"

Sandcastle kings with moats so grand,
A seagull swoops; it claims the land.
A treasure map, or so they thought,
Just marked the place where fish were caught.

As surfers glide, they flip and twirl,
Saltwater crowns, they dance and swirl.
"Catch that wave, don't wipe out, bob!
You'll land face-first, just like a slob!"

In salty air, with giggles loud,
The ocean's riddles gather a crowd.
Each splash a laugh, each tide a story,
In life's great sea of endless glory.

The Lighthouse Keeper's Diary

Atop the rocks, his lantern glows,
A keeper waits, where no one goes.
His diary filled with silly dreams,
Of mermaids dancing, or so it seems.

Each night he writes, "A ship I spied,
With a parrot perched, who squawked and lied!"
The foghorn's honk, his blaring friend,
"Don't call me late, until the end!"

The gulls complain, they seek their share,
"Is that a boat or your wild hair?"
With coffee strong and jokes to share,
He keeps the light, with love and care.

So here's to nights by the sea's grand sway,
With laughter echoing at the end of the day.
The lighthouse stands, a beacon bright,
With tales of joy, under moonlight.

The Land Where the Sea Meets the Sky

Where seagulls dance and dolphins play,
The sun winks down, hurraying the day.
Sandcastles topple, splashing with glee,
As children squeal in their sand-covered spree.

A crab in a tux, with his claws held high,
Chases a flip-flop that's daring to fly.
The ocean waves giggle, tickling your toes,
While we all shout, "Look! A fish with a nose!"

Kites soar above, swirling like dreams,
Pulled by the wind with jubilant screams.
Castles of sand, a sight to behold,
But watch out for tides that can be quite bold!

So here we laugh, by the shore we play,
In the land where the sea makes its sway.
With laughter unbridled, we'll frolic and run,
Creating our stories 'til day is done.

Secrets Hidden in Tide Pools

In the crevices where water dreams,
Tiny fish wiggle, busting at seams.
Anemones wave in a colorful trance,
While snails in their shells do a slow-motion dance.

Hermit crabs peek with a curious glare,
Wearing old shells as they shuffle with flair.
A starfish flaunts, claiming turf like a boss,
While barnacles gossip, not caring for loss.

The tide rolls in, a thundering cheer,
"Look at my treasures and creatures so dear!"
With each little splash, a giggle erupts,
As seaweed tickles, and laughter erupts.

So next time you're near, take a scoop and a glance,
In these little worlds where sea critters prance.
With secrets aplenty that life can bestow,
Each pool is a gem that sparkles and glows.

The Azure Riddle of the Sea

In depths of blue where mysteries hide,
The fish plot mischief, oh what a ride!
Octopuses laugh with eight arms spread wide,
While turtles glide like they're on a joyride.

A whale tells a joke with a splash and a spray,
While schools of bright fish swim their ballet.
"Why did the clam never share any sand?"
"Because he was a tad bit too unhandy!"

A treasure chest grins, painted bright gold,
With gemstones that sparkle, but it's more than old.
"Just keep your distance," the pirate warns me,
As he squawks out a song all about the sea.

With humor dripping from the ocean's heart,
Each wave brings a giggle, a world set apart.
So dive into laughter where shadows play tricks,
In the azure abyss, where the ocean's a mix.

Beneath Waves of Time

Under the surface, where stories are brewed,
Fish gossip in bubbles, oh how they're glued.
"Did you hear about the whale with no flair?"
"Yeah, he's the one who couldn't find his pair!"

Seashells are gossiping, who's in the know,
As waves whisper secrets, ebbing to and fro.
A dugong's snicker echoes through the blue,
While a crab, with a wink, sends a wink too.

Barnacles chuckle as they hold on tight,
To boats rocking gently in the moonlight.
With every tide shift, a prankster is born,
In a realm where the silly eats starfruit by dawn.

So take a dip where the water is fine,
In the realm of the goofy, where we intertwine.
Beneath waves of laughter, come join the spree,
In a sea full of whimsy, come dive in with me.

Secrets of the Seashell

A seashell said with a sly little grin,
"I once was a fish, now I'm here to spin!"
"I've seen all the waves and the tales they weave,
But don't tell the crabs, they won't believe!"

With tides that swirl and winds that sing,
Seashells gossip about everything.
They chuckle and laugh as the birds fly high,
While octopuses just roll their eyes and sigh.

Down by the shore, where the seaweed sways,
The critters conspire on these sunny days.
The snails tell secrets in their slimy tracks,
While starfish throw parties, and nobody lacks!

So if you find a shell, give it a listen,
You might hear tales that make you start whistlin'.
For in the ocean's hold, where laughter flows free,
There's humor aplenty, come join the spree!

Across the Horizon's Whispers

Across the horizon where the seabirds caw,
Lies a world of nonsense and whimsical awe.
With fishes in tuxedos and seahorses prance,
They've got oceanic plans for a fanciful dance.

The crabs play poker, they bluff with their claws,
While dolphins tell jokes that earn watery applause.
With laughter so loud, the waves take a peek,
As mermaids yell, "Hey, we've hit our peak!"

A pirate with parrot, a curious pair,
Tried to steal treasure, but found only hair!
While jellyfish glow like pixelated stars,
They glide through the water like silly loose cars.

In this seaside circus of giggles and light,
The crustaceans chuckle, oh what a sight!
So cast out your lines, let the good times ensue,
For laughter's the catch that belongs to you!

The Mariner's Lore

Gather 'round sailors, I've stories galore,
Of mermaids mistaken for fish at the shore.
With barnacles betting on who will win,
At the annual race where the clowns wear fins!

With tales of the cod that danced through the foam,
And barnacle geese who claimed the sea home.
The gulls cheered them on as they spun in the tide,
While the fish shouted, "Wait, we're not on that ride!"

The captain was crazy, lost treasure for sure,
When he followed a treasure map drawn by a boar.
But there's humor in folly, so they all had a laugh,
As waves washed the map from the boat's wooden shaft.

So hoist up your sails and let's all have a cheer,
For laughter's the bounty, all sailors hold dear!
The ocean's full of folly, just roll with the waves,
And together we'll cherish the life of the braves!

Dances of the Distant Pelagics

Oh what a party in the depths of the sea,
Where fishes don hats, looking fancy and free.
The mackerel waltz with the squid in a spin,
While the octopus claps with its eight floppy fins.

The turtles roll in with a laid-back style,
Teaching fish how to groove with an ancient smile.
A blowfish might puff up to take center stage,
While the anglerfish flickers a light for the page.

Under moonlit glow, they slide and they slide,
As the starfish boogie with great ocean pride.
The laughter erupts in the bubbles that rise,
As seahorses tango in their tiny ties.

So don your best fins and join in the fun,
For every fish knows it's a dance, never done!
In the dazzling deep where the water-sprites play,
Life's a comedy at the end of the day!

The Language of the Pebbles

Pebbles chat beneath my feet,
A gossiping crowd, oh what a treat!
They tell of waves that tease and play,
Whispers of sand from yesterday.

One says the crabs are planning a dance,
While shells giggle at their own romance.
A rock claims it's quite the heavy-weight,
But I swear it's just a bit irate.

They roll and tumble in the sun,
Each with stories, bursting with fun.
From tides that tickle to moonlit beams,
It's a stony world spun from dreams.

So next time you stroll by the shore,
Listen closely, it's never a bore.
For each little pebble has something to say,
In their joyful chatter, they brighten the day.

Tempests and Tranquility

When tempests rage and waves do clash,
The sharks swim by with a cheeky splash.
They laugh as sailors tie up their boats,
And sea turtles roll like whimsical goats.

But once the storm clouds drift away,
Tranquility beckons, come out and play.
A seagull drops by with a joke or two,
As dolphins dance in the sparkling blue.

Even the octopus joins in the fun,
Inking the water, yes, just for a pun.
While jellyfish float, looking bewildered,
In this comedy show, they feel quite shielded.

With laughter echoing through the waves,
Each splash a giggle, the ocean behaves.
From tempests wild to calm, sweet delight,
The sea keeps us chuckling day and night.

The Gulls' Secret Songs

High above, the gulls take flight,
With secret songs that bring delight.
They squawk of fish in curly fries,
And share their dreams 'neath sunny skies.

One gull thinks he's a tenor bright,
He serenades the stars at night.
While others chirp tales of lost bread crust,
As waves roll in, it's laughter they trust.

They hold a concert, twirling around,
With synchronized dives that astound.
A kid throws fries—oh what a sight!
The gulls dive down in comedic flight.

So if you hear a raucous cheer,
Just look up high, the show is near.
For at the shore, with skies so strong,
The gulls unite in their funny song.

Dreams Adrift in the Current

Drifting dreams on currents flow,
A beach ball rolls, with nowhere to go.
A starfish sings, its voice a delight,
As crabs do the cha-cha, holding on tight.

A lost flip-flop holds a debate,
With a seaweed carpet on its fate.
They ponder deep how to break free,
While seahorses giggle, sipping their tea.

The tide tickles shells, oh what a tease!
With whispers of fish that swim with ease.
A conch shell boasts of being the best,
While snails take a break, just to rest.

In this world where laughter is found,
With each wave's splash, a joy unbound.
Dreams adrift in a funny embrace,
On the ocean's surface, we dance and trace.

Shores of the Forgotten

On a sandy beach, crabs put on a show,
They dance in a line, with nowhere to go.
A seagull swoops down, a feathered buffoon,
It steals their snacks and hums a silly tune.

A flip-flop floats by like a lost little boat,
Mysterious treasures, oh what could they quote?
The tide rolls in laughter, waves tickling the sands,
"Who needs a compass when you've got your hands?"

Old bottles whisper secrets from ages long past,
While jellyfish wobbles, glowing like a cast.
A sailor's hat tips in a gust of pure glee,
"Adventure! Oh wait! Is that a crab next to me?"

So raise up your cups of saltwater and cheer,
For life on the shore, oh it's nothing to fear.
With giggles and splashes, we frolic and play,
On shores forgotten, come join the parade!

Beyond the Reach of Time

In a misty cove where shadows do tarry,
Time ticks away like a sly little fairy.
The old shipwreck grins, with barnacles bright,
"Who needs a captain? We'll sail on tonight!"

A starfish held court, with a crown made of kelp,
Telling wild stories, with a wink and a yelp.
"I once wrestled a seal, oh, what a grand fight!
He tickled my belly, we laughed 'til the night!"

The tides, they giggle, as the hours float past,
With dolphins in tutus, they swim in a blast.
Each wave brings a chuckle, each splash brings a cheer,
The ocean's great laughter, the sound we all hear.

No clocks here to bind us, no worries, no haste,
Just dancing and splashing, life's joys we embrace.
So come join the fun, in this timeless escape,
Where laughter and ocean, together take shape!

A Lantern's Gaze into the Abyss

A lantern hangs low, its light winks and beams,
Illuminating fish with glittering dreams.
A flounder whispers, "What's on for tonight?"
"Not much," says a crab, "just a crab-apple fight!"

In the depths of the dark, a lawyer fish waits,
With a briefcase of clams, negotiating fates.
"Sign here," he declares, "for a fine pinch of glee,
And I'll throw in a seaweed for free!"

A squid spills ink, with a flourish and flair,
"Who needs a pen when you're floating in air?"
The sunken ship gurgles, a sponge in a hat,
Acting quite fancy, though it's really quite flat.

So beam down your lanterns, let's party till dawn,
With sea critters laughing, all worries are gone.
In the abyss of the night, where giggles exist,
A lantern's bright glow makes for a change in the mist!

Conch Shell Chronicles

A conch shell sits proud, with stories galore,
It murmurs and chuckles from its sandy shore.
"Once I knew a crab with a hat and a cane,
He danced on the beach in the pouring rain!"

The clams gossip gently, with pearls to bestow,
"Did you hear about Jimmy? He just learned to flow!"
A wave crashes softly, "My stories are whacky,
Like the time I surfed with a whale that was wacky!"

A fish with a mustache joins in on the fun,
"Life under the sea, oh it's never quite done.
With laughter and stories, our days never cease,
Just don't ask the octopus; he'll talk Greek, at least!"

So gather your conch shells, their chronicle tales,
Of wobbly dolphins and fish that wear veils.
In laughter and splendor, the sea sings its rhyme,
Conch shell chronicles, a joy sublime!

Echoes of the Distant Shore

A crab in a tux, oh what a sight,
Dancing on sand under the moonlight.
Seagulls squawk in a jazzy tune,
While starfish twirl beneath the dune.

The tide pulls back, oh what a tease,
Shells gather round, trying to please.
A clam took a selfie, but it won't share,
Caught in a filter, with messy hair.

Mussels mingle, each with a tale,
As jellyfish float, wearing a veil.
Fish gossip, whispering with a grin,
'No need for a boat, the fun's here within!'

Under the sun, laughter does soar,
A riot of colors, the ocean's core.
So grab a shell, join this parade,
At the beach, our jokes won't fade!

Moonlit Symphony of the Tides

Crab orchestra tuning on the rocks,
Clams, shushed, trying to steal the clocks.
A fish on a trumpet plays quite rude,
While the squid gets tangled in its food.

Seashells debating who sings the best,
A starfish claims it's him, but what a jest!
With waves clapping hands, the ocean sways,
As dolphins mock with their playful ways.

Under the stars, the night feels alive,
Mermaids giggle as they dive and jive.
'Throw in a seaweed wig!' one exclaims,
In this moonlit symphony, no one's to blame.

So sway with the rhythm, dance with the tide,
Each bubble bursts laughing as we glide.
We're all a part of this watery play,
Where mirth and mischief come out to play!

The Siren's Lament

A siren sings, but the tune's a flop,
Caught in a loop, no rhythm to stop.
She yearns for a sailor, but finds no catch,
Just a rubber duck, in quite the patch.

'Oh sailor, come quick!' she cries with glee,
But all that replies is a bumbling bee.
Her hair all a tangle, she twists and twirls,
Wishing for romance with hunky swirls.

Fish rolling their eyes, boredom's their plight,
They launch a seaweed, oh what a sight!
The crab cheers her on, 'Try a new song!'
With a flipper or two, she can't go wrong.

Strumming her harp made of driftwood and dreams,
She hums a new ditty, or so it seems.
Her voice now a chuckle, the ocean just grins,
When the sea laughs with her, everyone's wins!

Driftwood Dreams

Driftwood sprawled like a fancy chair,
Hosts underwater parties without a care.
Starfish in hats, and fish in ties,
While crabs serve snacks, oh what a surprise!

They play underwater charades, quite absurd,
Mussels get stuck, and their voices slurred.
A seagull peeks down, looking for food,
While dolphins dive in with their joyful mood.

Bubbles of laughter rise to the sky,
With a twist and a spin, the sea creatures fly.
The octopus juggles, a sight that astounds,
In this driftwood dream where no one drowns.

So come join the fun, let your worries drift,
Join in the laughter, it's quite the gift.
With each wave that crashes, life is just grand,
At the edge of the ocean where dreams expand!

Sailors' Memories in the Wind

The captain lost his trusty hat,
But still he swore, he'd wear it—fat!
A parrot squawked, "A pirate's life!"
And winked at all the sailors' strife.

They danced on deck in stormy weather,
Twirling ropes like they were feathers.
The fish below rolled their beady eyes,
As sailors sang of lost supplies.

With every wave, a hearty laugh,
Their tales grew tall, like coral aft.
The jellyfish glowed, seemed to cheer,
For all the fun that drew them near.

And when the night began to fall,
They played a tune, a sea shanty call.
The stars above twinkled in sync,
As sailors raised their mugs to drink!

The Color of Distant Horizons

The sea was blue, a curious hue,
As dolphins danced and waved to you.
A sailor slipped on a slippery deck,
And earned a laugh, then went on to check.

The waves were painted, orange and gold,
While octopuses tangled in tales bold.
They wore bright caps, a fashion crime,
A sight so funny, you'd think it prime!

A mermaid giggled with hair so wild,
While hiding pearls, like a playful child.
The horizon winks with colors bright,
As fish wine-glass toast under starlit night.

And when the sun began to set,
Sailor jokes were quite the best bet.
For in that moment, laughter spread,
As waves took all their worries and dread.

Stardust Beneath the Waves

Beneath the waves, where stardust swirls,
A sea cucumber wore pearls and twirls.
The crabs all laughed, they called him 'Star',
While jellyfish floated near, not far.

A fish named Bob wore goggles bright,
Claiming he'd swim beyond the night.
He splashed and flopped, had quite a spree,
Spouting bubbles of sheer glee!

The seaweed danced with a funky beat,
And all the minnows felt the heat.
They formed a band, with shells for drums,
And played all night till morning comes.

So if you dive and look around,
In this fun world, joy can be found.
For stardust giggles float like dreams,
In oceans deep, or so it seems!

Melodies of the Mariner's Heart

The mariner sang to the ghostly breeze,
Of ships that sailed with utmost ease.
His tune brought forth a swell of mirth,
For laughter bubbled out from the earth.

With ukulele in a fanciful way,
He serenaded fishes each passing day.
Guitar-strummed waves joined the brightest song,
As gulls flew by and danced along.

A lobster clapped with such delight,
As sea turtles joined in the night.
Each pitch and roll, a hearty cheer,
Echoed across where waves drew near.

So if you hear a melody near,
Don't be surprised if it's a seafaring cheer.
For mariners know, with laughter so true,
That joy on the ocean is made for two!

The Siren's Lament

Once upon a rocky shore,
A siren sang but missed her score.
Her voice was sweet but quite off beat,
The fish all laughed, dance on their feet.

She tried to catch a sailor's eye,
But tripped on seaweed - oh my, oh my!
With every note, her hair would twirl,
And crabs would dance in a silly whirl.

When storms would come, she'd squeal with glee,
Jumping waves with a giggling spree.
While sailors clung to their ships so tight,
She'd make a splash, a frothy delight.

Oh, siren dear, with a laugh so loud,
Turned to a fish, she just feels proud.
With fins that flop, and scales that shine,
She rules the waves, with humor divine.

Fables in the Foam

Upon the crest of bubbling tides,
A whale recounted, with laughter, his rides.
'Twas once a kraken, misunderstood,
Who just wanted hugs, to feel good!

A sea turtle shared tales of woe,
When seagulls stole snacks, oh no, no, no!
With each little splash, around the coral,
They giggled and blushed, quite jovial moral.

Starfish played poker on the sandy floor,
While octopuses cooked, oh, what a bore!
Lobsters would clank their claws with pride,
In underwater bars, side by side.

So gather 'round, hear the ocean's jest,
For in the waves, humor's at its best.
With tales that flow like the swell and spray,
The ocean's laughter lingers all day.

Driftwood Dreams

On a plank of driftwood, dreams took flight,
Seagulls squawked tales in the morning light.
An old crab claimed he once knew a king,
But all he really had was a broken shell ring.

A tiny fish swam with flair and sass,
Chasing shadows, in the undersea grass.
He swore his reflection was quite a sight,
Though all he saw was a splash of fright.

Starfish played tricks on the unsuspecting,
While jellyfish danced, all gleaming, reflecting.
With each little wave, the fun would expand,
A party of critters, a lively band.

So dream on driftwood, embrace the cheer,
For in every current, there's joy to endear.
With laughter and silliness, nature's delight,
The ocean's heart beats, ever so bright.

Songs of the Stormy Sea

When the winds would howl like a playful beast,
The dolphins would gather and hold a feast.
With splashes and jumps, they'd serenade,
While raindrops danced, in a merry parade.

A gull with a hat, oh what a sight!
Swooped down to sing through the stormy night.
His tune cracked the clouds, made thunder grin,
As waves clapped back with a frothy win.

A clam shared secrets of treasure chests,
While a lobster recounted his fashion quests.
With tales so rich, they'd laugh and play,
Through tempestuous skies, brighter than day.

So raise a glass of briny beer,
To the songs of the sea that we hold dear.
For when the storms come, and the waves rock free,
We find our fun in the salty spree.

The Ocean's Grief

A crab in a suit, quite dapper and neat,
Stumbles around on his tiny little feet.
He tried to dance, but he tripped on a shell,
Now he's the talk of the tidepool, oh well!

A whale told a joke, but nobody laughed,
His punchline sank deeper than fishy old craft.
Fish rolled their eyes, and the dolphins just sighed,
While seagulls flew by, not impressed and pre-occupied.

The jellyfish laughed, floating gleefully round,
While octopuses twirled in their own sea sound.
A clam dropped its pearls, oh what a big fuss,
'Twas a gem of a blunder, now look what we've lost!

But under the waves, where the seaweed does sway,
The ocean can't cry—it's just seawater play.
With bubbles of giggles and foam flying free,
It's a watery kingdom, where silliness glees!

Incantations of the Saltwater Muse

An old sea turtle with wisdom to share,
Wove spells from the seaweed, conjured with flair.
He promised fresh sea cucumber for all,
But forgot the recipe—oops! What a fall!

A mermaid with glitter and seashells in hand,
Tried to charm the fish into forming a band.
But the trumpetfish blew in a crooked old way,
And the octopus thought he was here for ballet!

Starfish gathered, clapped with their tiny arms,
Hoping, just hoping, to catch all the charms.
But each time they danced, they got stuck in the sand,
Flipping and flopping in their own messy band!

Yet laughter arose from the depths of the brine,
As creatures performed their own silly design.
For magic is laughter, not just a sweet tune,
In the heart of the ocean, there's humor in bloom!

Silent Dunes and Murmuring Seas

The sand whispered secrets to each grain nearby,
While gulls squawked their gossip, oh me, oh my!
A crab in a top hat declared it his throne,
With a shell for a seat, he felt right at home!

The wind tickled dunes, tick-tock like a clock,
While beach balls rolled by like a playful rock.
An old pair of flip-flops argued all day,
"Left foot leads on!" "No! It's right foot's play!"

But the seashells just chuckled, each one with a grin,
At the dramas unfolding in the warm sea's din.
A kite's soared high, tangled in a sea breeze,
And a walrus slid in, doing belly-flop tease!

As the sun set low, painting skies bright and pink,
The ocean just giggled—"Let's not overthink!"
With laughter and joy spilling over the edge,
Let's gather our stories from the silty dredge!

Tides of the Lost Mariner

A mariner lost with maps upside down,
Set sail at sunrise, forgot his way 'round.
His compass was spinning, he'd followed a crab,
Now he's chasing fish tails—in a sailing slab!

With gusts of adventure and shanties so loud,
He danced on the deck, oh man, he was proud.
But waves rolled in swiftly, and he slipped with a splash,
Now he's just a fish whisperer, and a young sea-bash!

A seagull perched high, with a monocle on,
Watched all the antics while munching a prawn.
"Map's on the fridge!" it squawked, what a sight,
As the mariner bobbed underneath in delight!

And as the sun set with giggles and cheer,
Our lost sailor grinned—not a moment of fear.
For the sea tells us stories, both silly and grand,
In her whimsical waves, a fun-loving band!

The Salted Breath of Adventure

The seagulls squawked a curious tune,
As pirate hats danced under the moon.
With a treasure map made of ripped-up pie,
We chased after dreams, oh me, oh my!

An octopus sold us ice cream so sweet,
But it dripped all over our sandy feet.
We laughed till we snorted, what a grand sight,
Under the stars, our hearts felt so light.

Swimmers were yelling, 'Watch out for waves!'
While mermaids grinned, guarding their caves.
In flip-flops and goggles, we made our stance,
And joined in the ocean's wobbly dance.

With jellyfish winking, the fun never ends,
As crabby companions became our best friends.
Oh, the salted breath filled with laughter and cheer,
In this wacky world, there's nothing to fear!

Lullabies of the Coastal Breeze

The wind whispered secrets to shells on the shore,
While kids built castles, mighty and more.
A crab with a crown said, 'Bow to the king!'
In this sandy kingdom, laughter took wing.

Seashells chimed softly a musical tune,
At nightfall, they danced beneath the full moon.
With ice cream in hand, we swayed side to side,
While the waves giggled, grumbling and wide.

Fish in tuxedos swam past in a rush,
Chasing their tails in a wiggly hush.
They tossed seaweed hats and made us all cheer,
In every splash, a smile would endear.

The coastal breeze sang lullabies sweet,
As friends shared their giggles and salty ice treats.
In this wild place, where joy knows no end,
Forever we'll cherish the waves and their friends.

Legends Carried by the Currents

A fish with a monocle claimed he could tell,
Of pirate gold buried just off the swell.
We followed the currents, excited and bold,
In search of the treasure, our stories retold.

But lo and behold, it was just a big rock,
Covered in seaweed, it did mock and mock!
The crab waved his claws; 'Do not be so glum!'
The real prize was laughter—we knew it would come.

The dolphins burst forth, putting on a show,
While flip-flopping seals joined them below.
With every wave crashing, our spirits would rise,
In this ocean of giggles, we found our surprise.

So legends may fade, but the joy holds tight,
In every splash, we'll find pure delight.
With shouts and with cheers, the adventure was grand,
There's magic, you see, in the sea and the sand.

Shadows on the Sand

With shadows of pirates playing tag in the tide,
We ran and we jumped, full of giggles and pride.
Ghost stories whispered by waves in the night,
As the moon painted silver our hearts full of light.

A whale in a top hat danced with a fish,
Making wishes come true with a single swish.
We stomped in the puddles and splashed all around,
In the glow of the moonlight, adventure was found.

Seagulls flapping wildly, performing a show,
As shells made their music, a shimmering flow.
Oh, how we laughed, at the things we had planned,
In this magical world, where shadows took stand.

As night wore on lightly, our dreams drifted near,
In the whispers of breezes, we had nothing to fear.
For tomorrow would come with new tales to expand,
And shadows and laughter would fill up the sand.

Destinies in the Dunes

In sandcastles built with flair,
A crab tried to take my chair.
He danced with a towel, oh what a sight,
I couldn't help but laugh in delight.

Seagulls squawked with a mischievous grin,
One stole my fries and dove right in.
With sandy shoes and seaglass galore,
Who knew the beach held such folklore?

Beneath the Sailor's Solitude.

A sailor named Fred, with one eye of blue,
Told fishy tales that made no sense, too.
His parrot squawked jokes, loud as a drum,
While fish in the sea just rolled in the scum.

His boat was a float, held up by good luck,
And a mermaid came by, with a jealous duck.
They argued for hours about the best bait,
While laughter erupted, it truly was great.

Whispers of the Seafoam

The seafoam whispered secrets sweet,
To beachcombers dancing on vibrant feet.
A jellyfish jiggled, a sight quite bizarre,
While starfish played cards under a nearby star.

Turtles raced past, wearing big hats,
With sunglasses on, looking quite phat.
The ocean's a circus, full of jest,
And every wave brings a new kind of quest.

Secrets Beneath the Waves

Bubbles rose up with a giggle and glee,
Fish telling secrets, as bold as can be.
A lobster faced off with a crab in a duel,
The audience cheered, who knew they were cool?

A whale's belly laughed, or so it was said,
He told all the stories that rocked in his head.
From sunken ships to a pirate's last feast,
The ocean's a vault where the funny never ceased.

Currents of Forgotten Legends

In seas where mermaids dance and play,
The fish have secrets, or so they say.
A crab once wore a crown too tight,
He ruled the shore for one wild night.

The octopus juggles shells and foam,
While seagulls squawk, they're far from home.
A dolphin laughs at a surfer's fall,
The waves applaud, oh, nature's call!

The treasure chest is full of junk,
A rusty key and a lone sock's funk.
The sunken ship has tales untold,
But mostly just seaweed and old gold.

So gather round and share a grin,
For ocean mischief is about to begin.
With salty air and waves so grand,
The ocean's humor, we all understand.

Beneath the Azure Canopy

Beneath the dazzling azure skies,
A seagull swoops with clever eyes.
It steals a chip from a picnicker's hand,
While giggles erupt, oh, isn't it grand?

A jellyfish floats with a goofy grin,
As beachgoers build their castles of sin.
The tide comes in to sweep them away,
They laugh and shout, 'Let's start a new day!'

With crabs in tuxedos, marching in line,
They strut on the sand, thinking they shine.
A clam opens wide with a big surprise,
A pearl that's not real—oh, what a guise!

So under the sun, let hilarity reign,
As seaweed dances, a merry refrain.
To kick up some sand, and cheer with delight,
For laughter and joy, from morning to night.

The Call of the Distant Horizon

On the horizon, sailboats roam,
But one just drifted too far from home.
The captain yells, 'Where are we, mate?'
'Just follow the gulls!' was fate's own bait.

A whale performs with a diving show,
While fish nearby giggle, 'What a pro!'
The anchors are tangled, the crew in a spin,
As laughter erupts from the blunders within.

The compass spins in a cheeky dance,
Leading the way with a playful chance.
They find an island with peculiar snacks,
Sandwiches made from bright green kelp packs!

So raise a toast to the sea's gentle jest,
For every journey, it's truly the best.
With waves that chuckle and winds that sing,
Adventure awaits, let the fun bells ring!

Beneath the Salt-Kissed Skies

Beneath the salt-kissed skies so blue,
The gulls squawk loudly, 'What's new with you?'
A starfish dreams of swimming with flair,
While a crab tries to dance in midair.

A picnic spread, with treats galore,
But ants invade; it's quite the uproar.
Shrimp gossiping about human snacks,
They relish the chaos, enjoy the laughs.

The beach ball bounces, a race to the waves,
A splash fight erupts—how each one behaves!
With laughter a-plenty and sunscreen galore,
They build up their stories, and spirits soar.

So let's all gather, and share the delight,
For every sunset heralds a night.
With seaweed crowns and friends at our side,
Beneath these skies, we'll forever abide.

Elysium Beneath the Waves

Bubbles in the sea, fishy and bright,
A crab with a grin starts a dance at night.
"Come join me!" he squeaks, with a jiggly sway,
While dolphins spin tales, in a quirky ballet.

Octopuses juggle, without any fuss,
They slip and they slide, on a clammy bus.
"Catch me if you can!" shouts a fish in a dash,
As seaweed gets tangled in a big, funny splash.

A seagull drops snacks, with a jubilant clack,
While turtles roll over, and give a loud quack.
The starfish all chuckle at the fun they see,
In a world full of giggles beneath the sea.

So join in the frolic, take a splashy ride,
With the creatures of laughter, nowhere to hide.
For laughter is bountiful, floating on waves,
In this underwater fun, where whimsy behaves.

Dreams on the Windward Coast

Seagulls play tag in the bright morning air,
While fishermen giggle, no worries or care.
They cast out their lines with a flick and a flip,
But catch only seaweed and a very lost ship.

A crab named Louie with a top hat and cane,
Stumbles on rocks, but gets up once again.
"Excuse me, dear fish, have you seen my parade?"
The fish roll their eyes, in a sweet, fishy charade.

Waves crash with laughter, they tickle the shore,
Chasing sandcastles, oh, what a chore!
The beach ball goes flying, a dog gets the blame,
While kids shout with joy, playing their silly game.

So dance on the beach, let your worries go free,
Where dreams are as light as a fluttering sea.
With the wind in your hair, it's pure seaside cheer,
At the coast where all laughter just loves to appear.

The Dance of the Sea Foam

Sea foam has parties, when the tide is just right,
It bubbles and dances, in the pale moonlight.
"Join us!" they giggle, as waves start to swirl,
The mermaids all cheer, with a flip and a twirl.

A clam plays the trumpet, a shrimp on drums,
The fish start to flutter, with their flippers and thumbs.
"Let's do the sea shuffle!" yells a squishy old squirt,
A snail spins gracefully, without a single hurt.

The jellies glow bright, like lanterns afloat,
While a seal cracks jokes, that make everyone gloat.
"Why didn't the dolphin take the school bus?" he jokes,
"Because he was too busy with the aquatic blokes!"

So next time you're near, listen close to the tide,
For the sea foam's laughter you simply can't hide.
It's a nightly affair, full of glee and delight,
In the dance of the waves, kissing the night.

Reflections of the Setting Sun

Goldfish gather 'round as the sun sinks low,
They share silly stories, in the warm evening glow.
"Remember that time when we chased that big boat?"
The tales get exaggerated, nobody can gloat.

The ocean whispers secrets, to the shells on the shore,
While crabs in tuxedos perform dance moves galore.
"Raise your pincers high!" croons a jellyfish band,
As they serenade sunsets on the sparkly sand.

Starfish keep score of the highest of leaps,
While muskrat's in stitches, rolling over in heaps.
The laughter spreads wide, like the tide's gentle hum,
As the sea becomes playground for all that's to come.

So as twilight unfolds, let your worries be spun,
In the mirth of the moment, beneath the setting sun.
With giggles and chuckles echoing around,
The ocean holds treasures in joy that abound.

Myths Among the Sea Grass

In the depths where seaweed sways,
Mermaids lost in silly plays,
Jellyfish dance with goofy glee,
Laughing with all their fishy spree.

A crab in a hat, with a bright red bow,
Tells tales of a shark's ballet show,
He spins and twirls, a comical sight,
Leaving the dolphins in pure delight.

The octopus juggles shells with skill,
While clownfish giggle, giving a thrill,
The starfish claps with a floppy cheer,
Creating a scene that's sunny and clear.

So dive in deep, let your worries flee,
Join in the fun, come splash in the sea,
For among the waves where the laughter does creep,
The ocean's a stage, where silliness leaps.

The Sailor's Scroll

A sailor once wrote with a quill so grand,
Of sea monsters dancing, just like he planned,
With a kraken that flips pancakes each morn,
And a dolphin that plays on a horn.

He scribbled of fish with game show dreams,
Spinning in circles, creating bright schemes,
A seagull who sings while juggling some fries,
With a wink and a squawk, oh what a surprise!

Rumors of treasure hidden so well,
Only found by a clam that can spell,
Though most just end up, lost in the tide,
Chasing their tails, with nowhere to hide.

So grab your compass, let's set out to sea,
For tales of the funny are waiting for thee,
With each salty wave, let laughter prevail,
In a sailor's grand scroll, there's always a tale.

Below the Surface

Beneath the waves, where the bubbles rise,
Lives a fish who's taken a fifth in disguise,
He wears tiny glasses, reads books every day,
Making friends with a snail who is wise in her way.

An eel with a perm sways to the beat,
While sea cucumbers groove on their feet,
The turtles are taking a yoga class,
As laughter erupts, a delightful morass.

The crustaceans gossip in their coral café,
Trading tall tales while sipping cold bray,
A clam, remarkably, invented a joke,
And the laughter grows louder until it provokes.

So plunge down below, where the fun's never far,
With secrets and giggles, just follow the star,
In this underwater world, where nonsense is gold,
A treasure of laughter, so joyful and bold.

Between the Stars

Under a sky where the sea meets the night,
Shimmering fish share their dreams in twilight,
A starfish on a mission, to count every star,
While a whale sings softly, 'You won't get too far!'

A rocket ship made from driftwood and shells,
Takes off with a crew where the laughter compels,
The jellybeans giggle, floating so free,
As they sparkle and dance in celestial glee.

The seagulls compete in a race through the air,
With octopuses cheering, waving with flair,
Each splash of the wave whispers secrets untold,
In a cosmic embrace, where irony's bold.

So gaze at the sky, let your spirit soar,
Amongst all the wonders, there's always room for more,
Under the moonlight, where giggles ignite,
Between twinkling stars, everything feels right.

The Keeper of the Coastal Secrets

There lies a beach, where secrets are spun,
The keeper collects them, each day's just begun,
With shells full of laughter and sandcastles tall,
She sprinkles the joy, like confetti, for all.

The seashore's a canvas, where crabs paint their dreams,
With buckets of giggles and sunshiney beams,
The dolphins perform circus tricks so divine,
While seahorses trot in a fanciful line.

The wind whispers tales of the funny and grand,
As the sun dips below, the skies start to band,
Flipping each secret like a pancake unturned,
Each laugh adds the warmth of a world that has churned.

So visit her realm, and you'll surely find,
Stories aplenty, good humor entwined,
For the keeper of secrets, oh how she knows,
That laughter's the tide, for it always just flows.

Heartbeats of the Deep

Inky squids dance with bubbles,
Tickling fish with bright, wobbly troubles.
A crab in a tux, looking quite spry,
Waves a claw with a wink in his eye.

Coral reefs giggle at passing whales,
As dolphins spin funny little tales.
A starfish tries on a sailor's cap,
But trips on a seaweed, oh what a flap!

Seagulls squawk jokes from the sky so blue,
While a clam reads poems, who knew it could do?
Pirate parrots crack up, rolling on fins,
Rescue a mermaid with mismatched twin fins!

Under the surface, there's laughter galore,
Crustaceans unite for a sea floor encore.
Bubbles of joy pop and hiss in delight,
As fish hold a party that lasts through the night.

Journey of the Wandering Starfish

A starfish strolls with its five little points,
Searching for snacks in the seaweed joints.
It trips over sandcastles made by a crab,
Who grumps and declares, "You're breaking my lab!"

It floats on a wave that tickles its arms,
Chasing a turtle with charming fish charms.
"Oh, what a life, just drifting about,
No worries, no deadlines, no need to freak out!"

But soon a sea urchin blocks all the fun,
"Step over me? You think I'm a pun?"
The starfish nods and laughs with a grin,
"I'm just passing through, not wanting to spin!"

A dolphin joins in with a flip and a splash,
While the jellyfish giggles—oh, what a clash!
With laughter and jests as they swim on their way,
Nothing beats friendship at the end of the day.

Breezes from Forgotten Isles

On shores of sand where the palm trees lean,
A crab flips a burger, it's quite a scene!
The seagulls are sous chefs, cawing with zest,
"Bring on the waves, and we'll host the best fest!"

Shells on the beach shimmy and shake,
As the wind whispers secrets, make no mistake.
A lighthouse stands tall, cracking its jokes,
While the waves chuckle back like friendly folks.

Coconut drinks flow with colorful straws,
While turtles in sunglasses applaud with their claws.
The sun sets in style, a curtain of gold,
A party of critters, so funny and bold!

As night drapes its cloak, the stars start to hum,
A serenade from the ocean, a jubilant drum.
So here on the edge, where laughter takes flight,
The breezes bring joy, wrapping us tight.

The Sunken Treasure's Song

Down where the pirates once buried their gold,
A mermaid hums songs, forever retold.
With a glittering smile, she calls out the crew,
"Join me for treasures, oh, what a view!"

Octopuses juggling their riches with glee,
While fish form a chorus, swimming carefree.
"Gold's just a hoax; it's the laughter we find,
In the depths of the ocean, all treasures unwind!"

A sunken ship sighs with stories to share,
While sea cucumbers nod, lost in their stare.
"Dig up the fun, let's see what we've got,
Not all that glitters is what we have sought!"

Bubbles burst forth like confetti from dreams,
As the tide carries whispers of giggles and screams.
So dance with the waves, let your heart catch the song,
For underwater laughter is where we belong!

Whispers of the Tides

A crab wore a mask at the party last night,
He danced with a fish, what a comical sight!
The shells held their breath, in a giggling line,
As seagulls recited their jokes from the brine.

A dolphin did cartwheels, quite proud of his tricks,
While the clownfish pretended to juggle with sticks.
The waves rolled in laughter, the tide gave a cheer,
For laughter was plenty, and nothing to fear.

An octopus juggled while sipping his tea,
With legs all a-wobble, oh what a spree!
The barnacles chuckled, stuck tight to the rocks,
As the starfish just smiled, counting his socks.

At sunset, the fun washed ashore with a splash,
As seashells exchanged all their secrets in HASH.
Under moonlight's glow, they all had a ball,
The ocean's great laughter, binding them all.

Secrets Beneath the Waves

A fish with a bowtie was quite out of place,
He tried to impress with his fancy fish grace.
A turtle was laughing, said, "Don't you know?"
"Underwater fashion's just for show!"

The clams paid in pearls for a ticket to see,
The bottom of the ocean's live comedy spree.
A seaweed comedian cracked jokes on the sand,
His punchlines so green, you just had to stand!

Two crabs with a plan tried to steal a nice snack,
But fell in a net—oh, what a comical whack!
With shrimp as their witnesses, how could they flee?
The sea laughed along, "Now that's rich, can't you see?"

When bubbles start rising, the ocean's all glee,
For laughter and mischief must always run free.
As the fish told their tales in the glow of the moon,
Secrets swirl down to the depths in a tune.

Echoes of Distant Shores

A gull with a hat claimed the pier as his own,
While the sea roared with laughter, quite overblown.
He squawked out a joke that was stolen from sea,
And the barnacles chuckled, "That's cringy, you see!"

The waves whispered softly, "Come join in our fun,
We'll splash with the dolphins till long after sun!"
With a splash and a giggle, they raced down the coast,
And the sand spoke its secrets, laughing the most.

A jellyfish wobbled, a spunky delight,
Spinning tales of mischief that glimmered all night.
"Watch out for my dance, it's a slippery whirl!"
The otters just chuckled, "Oh boy, what a twirl!"

As dusk settled in, they all gathered near,
Each wave brought a story, a hearty good cheer.
With echoes of laughter that filled up the sea,
The shores stood united, all happy and free.

Moonlit Stories of the Sea

The moon hung just right, casting shadows galore,
As fish held a banquet on the ocean floor.
"What's on the menu, just sand or some kelp?"
They giggled together, "How about some help?"

An eel made a joke about slimy good taste,
While octopuses sighed, "We're in quite a race!"
To find the best snacks as the sea foam would rise,
The laughter erupted beneath starry skies.

A zany old turtle rolled up with a grin,
Said, "I've got some tricks that will surely bring kin!"
The fish all reacted, with bubbles and twirls,
"For the longest of laughs, just watch how it swirls!"

With lanterns of light, they played all night long,
Each hour more laughter, their hearts felt so strong.
The moon winked above, casting glows on their fun,
In the depths of the sea, mischief's never done!

www.ingramcontent.com/pod-product-compliance
Lightning Source LLC
Chambersburg PA
CBHW050307120526
44590CB00016B/2522